Who Was
Alfred Hitchcock?

Who Was
Alfred Hitchcock?

by Pam Pollack and Meg Belviso

illustrated by Jonathan Moore

Penguin Workshop

For Peggy Thomson, Partner in Crime—PP

To Irene Meltzer Richard, Mistress of Suspense
at Lincoln Center—MB

For Betty, Char, Adam, and Mads—JM

PENGUIN WORKSHOP
An Imprint of Penguin Random House LLC, New York

Text copyright © 2014 by Pam Pollack and Meg Belviso.
Illustrations copyright © 2014 by Penguin Random House LLC. All rights reserved.
Published by Penguin Workshop, an imprint of Penguin Random House LLC, New York.
PENGUIN and PENGUIN WORKSHOP are trademarks of Penguin Books Ltd.
WHO HQ & Design is a registered trademark of Penguin Random House LLC.
Printed in the USA.

Visit us online at www.penguinrandomhouse.com.

Library of Congress Control Number: 2014958187

ISBN 9780448482378   10 9 8 7 6 5 4

Contents

Who Was
Alfred Hitchcock?

In the early 1900s, London, England, was a city full of crime. The officer on duty at the East End police station never knew who was going to come through the door. But one night when the door opened, he was quite surprised by what he saw.

It was a little boy, five or six years old. He was chubby and quiet and alone. His name was Alfred Hitchcock. With wide eyes, he approached the policeman and handed him a note.

In later years Alfred Hitchcock could not remember why he had been sent to the police station. He only knew that he had done something wrong at home. Perhaps he tracked mud through the house or didn't do his chores. Whatever it was, Alfred's father thought he needed to be taught a lesson about what happened when Alfred didn't behave.

So he wrote a note and sent Alfred to the local police station. He told him to give the note to the officer on duty.

Alfred watched, terrified, as the policeman read his father's note. Then the man took Alfred by the hand and led him into the station. For the first time in his life Alfred saw a jail cell. It had a big lock and iron bars. The policeman put Alfred in the cell and shut the door. He turned the lock with a big metal key.

Alfred gripped the bars with his tiny hands and pressed his round face against them.

The policeman looked down at him. "This is what we do to naughty boys," he said solemnly.

Then he walked away. The seconds ticked by. Alfred's heart was pounding. Would the man ever come back? Would Alfred be in jail forever?

Would he live on bread and water? Would anyone come and save him?

Just when Alfred was sure he would never see his mother again, the policeman returned. The child had only been in the jail cell for about five minutes. But it seemed like forever. The policeman opened the door and let Alfred out. He said he hoped the young boy had learned his lesson.

Alfred certainly had!

He would spend the rest of his life scaring movie audiences all over the world. When asked where he got his inspiration for such thrilling, scary stories, he always mentioned his time in jail.

Was the story made up, or was it true? No one can say for sure. Alfred Hitchcock claimed it really happened. But Alfred Hitchcock was a master storyteller.

Chapter 1
Call Me Hitch

Alfred Hitchcock was born on August 13, 1899. His brother, William, and sister, Nellie, were nine and seven. Alfred's father, William, ran a grocery store and his mother, Emma, took good care of the children. The family lived above the grocery store. Life at 517 High Road was very orderly.

From an early age, Alfred liked to be alone. At family gatherings he stood off in a corner watching everyone else. Although there were other children who lived on his street, Alfred always played by himself or watched the other children play. For him this was more fun than being with other people. By the time he was eight, Alfred had ridden all the tramlines in London. He had taken the river steamers all the way to the mouth of the Thames River! He loved to ride streetcars and big ships and kept charts of all their routes. He also memorized train timetables—the hours of all the arrivals and departures. To Alfred, keeping track of the schedules was as exciting as reading stories.

63	81	89	STATIONS		8	19
	6:10					
7:38	6:19		LONDON		7:45	8:00
7:47	6:28	5:58			7:58	8:11
7:59	6:36	6:04			8:09	8:21
8:10		6:12			8:16	8:29
8:19	6:54	6:20			8:30	8:37
8:28	7:06	6:28			8:38	8:45
8:36	7:15	6:39	LEBANON		8:46	8:56
8:45	7:23	6:48			8:59	9:06
8:54	7:32	6:56	MANSFIELD		9:10	
9:05	7:41	7:05	WILLINGTON		9:21	9:28
9:16	7:49	7:13			9:33	9:40
9:26	7:58	7:20			9:41	9:48
	8:06	7:29			9:50	9:56
9:44	8:16	7:38			10:00	
9:56	8:25	7:45				
	8:34	7:56				

Every evening Alfred's mother called him to
her room and asked him questions about his day.
He confided in her about everything he had seen
and heard.

At the time, movie theaters did not exist. But
the Hitchcock family loved to go to the theater
to see plays performed onstage. Alfred not only
enjoyed the stories and the characters but also the
way the lighting could make the audience react.

He remembered a show where the ghostly looking villain stood under a spooky green light. He was amazed at how a simple lighting trick made a character seem more frightening.

It sometimes seemed as if much of young Alfred's life was scary, too. One night he woke up and found the house empty. He went from room to room calling out for his parents. He didn't know it, but they had gone for a walk. His brother and sister weren't at home. Alfred was completely alone, and he was scared. He wandered around the empty house. There was "nothing but night" all around him. Later, his parents came home and found him in the kitchen crying.

In 1910 Alfred started school at St. Ignatius College, a Catholic school for boys. Alfred still liked to spend time alone. Years later, a classmate of his remembered him as a plump schoolboy leaning against the wall, his hands folded across his round stomach, simply watching the other boys.

ST. IGNATIUS COLLEGE

The Jesuit priests who were his teachers were strict, and punishments were harsh. And yet, Alfred still broke the rules. One of his favorite tricks was to steal eggs from the school henhouse. He liked to throw them at the windows of one of the teacher's homes. When the teacher asked him who did it, Alfred looked at the sky and shrugged. "I don't know, Father. It looks like the birds have been flying overhead."

This attitude earned him the nickname "Cocky" from the younger students. He hated the name almost as much as "Fred." That was what his parents called him. So Alfred Hitchcock chose a nickname for himself, the one by which he would be known for the rest of his life: "Hitch."

By the time he was fourteen, one of Hitch's favorite pastimes was sitting in on criminal trials at the famous Old Bailey courthouse.

He loved listening to the details of the court
cases, especially murder trials. Whenever he
could, he visited the Black Museum at Scotland
Yard.

THE BLACK MUSEUM

THE BLACK MUSEUM OPENED IN 1874.
TODAY IT IS HOUSED IN SCOTLAND YARD (THE
HEADQUARTERS OF THE METROPOLITAN POLICE IN
LONDON) AND IS OFFICIALLY CALLED THE CRIME
MUSEUM. IT HOUSES ITEMS AND EVIDENCE FROM
FAMOUS AND UNUSUAL CRIMES. IT WAS CREATED
TO HELP POLICE OFFICERS STUDY CRIME AND
CRIMINAL TACTICS. TODAY POLICE OFFICERS FROM
ALL OVER THE WORLD VISIT THE EXHIBITS, WHICH

INCLUDE A LETTER THOUGHT TO BE WRITTEN BY
JACK THE RIPPER. THE CRIME MUSEUM ALSO
CONTAINS NOOSES FROM EXECUTIONS, SWORDS
HIDDEN IN CANES, GUNS HIDDEN IN UMBRELLAS,
AND A COLLECTION OF COUNTERFEIT MONEY.

Alfred attended St. Ignatius College until he was fourteen. Then his parents sent him to the School of Engineering and Navigation. They hoped he would become an engineer, but he was much more interested in the latest entertainment to hit England—movies. There were four hundred movie screens in London by 1914,

visited by eighty thousand people weekly. That wasn't very much compared to the five million people who attended movies daily in the United States at that time. Movies hadn't quite caught on yet in England, but they had captured the attention of teenage Alfred Hitchcock.

Chapter 2
The Director's Chair

Alfred's father, William, worked long hours in the grocery store. He had difficulty breathing and later developed problems with his kidneys. When Alfred was only fifteen, his father died.

His brother, William Jr., no longer lived at home, and his sister was already married. Alfred left school and went to work to earn money for himself and his mother. Alfred also took photography and art classes at the University of London. He began reading film journals.

These were not fan magazines that gushed over stars; they were technical journals that explained how movies were made. Hitch preferred American films to British ones. American movies used backlighting—placing some of the light source behind the actors—which made the actors appear to stand out from the background. In British films everything looked flat. It wasn't so different from the lighting tricks he'd noticed on the stage as a young boy.

In 1920 the American film company Paramount announced that it was building a studio in London called Famous Players-Lasky. Alfred went to the office and showed them some of his drawings. He was given a job designing film title cards.

At this time there was no recorded sound—no audio track—for movies. All movies were silent. Any important information or dialogue was provided in words shown on the screen, called "titles."

The villain is aboard!

Alfred did so well drawing titles that he became head of the title department. From there he went to work in the editorial department, deciding what the titles should say. He studied American writers for tips on how to write scripts. When a director got sick, Hitch stepped in to help direct. He was learning all aspects of filmmaking.

Paramount's Famous Players-Lasky stopped making movies in England in 1923. The studio was then rented to British-owned film companies. One was run by Michael Balcon, who gave Hitch—as Alfred was now known—a job as an assistant director. Balcon asked

MICHAEL BALCON

Hitch who he thought he should hire to write scripts. Hitch offered to do it himself. He also volunteered to be the art director.

The one job he didn't take for himself was that of editor. For that he recommended a young woman he had worked with in the past: Alma Reville. The more Hitch worked with Alma, the more he liked her. They took a trip to Germany

to scout locations for a new film. On the way
home, Alma became seasick crossing the English
Channel. Hitch chose this moment to propose
to her. According to Hitch, Alma "groaned,

nodded her head, and burped." He said, "It
was one of my greatest scenes—a little weak on
dialogue, perhaps, but beautifully staged and not
overplayed."

By 1925 Hitch was writing scripts, creating sets, and assisting the director. The only job he had never done on his own was the most important one: director.

After years of learning nearly every job on a movie set, Alfred Hitchcock was finally ready to sit in the director's chair.

Chapter 3
The Silent Era

Hitch's first completed movie as a director, *The Pleasure Garden,* was about two friends who have some unlikely adventures in love. Michael Balcon sent Hitchcock, along with Alma, to Germany in 1925. The cameraman warned Hitch not to tell the border patrol that he was carrying film or cameras. He would have to pay German customs officers a fee to bring them into the country.

Hitch trembled and sweated as customs officials searched his train compartment. They didn't find the camera, but they took all the film. The next day, just as the cameraman arrived with twenty pounds of new film, their original film was returned. They had paid for twice as much film as they needed, and they still had to pay the customs fee on top of that. Hitch's first movie was already over budget, and he hadn't even begun filming!

Despite the problems, Hitch enjoyed working in Germany because German directors were making some of his favorite movies at that time. He liked the way the German filmmakers used shadows and strange scenery to tell fantastic, thrilling, and sometimes scary tales.

In the spring of 1926, Balcon found a story well suited to Hitch's interests. *The Lodger* was inspired by the true crimes of Jack the Ripper. Hitch and Alma worked out the details of the story together.

Hitch was quickly learning that his wife-to-be was a valuable collaborator.

When *The Lodger* was finished, it was shown to distributors who would consider booking it into their theaters. The head of the group, C. M. Woolf, said, "Your picture is so dreadful that we're just going to put it on a shelf and forget about it." Luckily for Hitch, a film critic convinced Mr. Woolf that the movie was good enough to release.

The Lodger showed British audiences a whole new kind of filmmaking, one that revealed information in very creative ways. In one famous scene, the family hears their lodger— the person to whom they've rented one of their spare bedrooms—pacing in his room above their heads. This was not easy to show in a silent movie. Without being able to hear the footsteps, how could the audience understand what was going on? Hitch used a glass floor in the lodger's bedroom so that the audience could see the

JACK THE RIPPER

JACK THE RIPPER TERRORIZED LONDON IN THE FALL OF 1888. HE KILLED FIVE WOMEN AND WAS NEVER CAUGHT. NO ONE KNOWS FOR SURE WHO HE WAS. *THE LODGER* WAS A STORY THAT BUILT SUSPENSE AND FEAR IN THE MINDS OF THE MOVIE AUDIENCE, JUST AS THE MYSTERIOUS AND UNKNOWN JACK THE RIPPER DID IN REAL LIFE.

DURING HIS CRIME SPREE, THE POLICE RECEIVED HUNDREDS OF LETTERS FROM PEOPLE CLAIMING TO BE JACK THE RIPPER. ALL BUT ONE IS CONSIDERED TO BE A FAKE. THAT SINGLE LETTER CAN BE FOUND IN THE BLACK MUSEUM AT SCOTLAND YARD.

character's feet moving back and forth, causing the chandelier to shake in the dining room below.

Hitchcock himself even appeared in the film as an extra—a person in the background—something he would continue to do for the rest of his career.

Hitch found he liked scaring audiences. He was fascinated by crime and criminals, and he had so many fears himself that scaring other people made him feel connected to them.

While Hitch and Alma waited for *The Lodger* to be released in movie theaters, they started their life together. Alma converted to Catholicism, and on December 2, 1926, they were married in London.

The Lodger opened in February 1927. It was a huge hit in Britain. People lined up around the block to see it. The public was even more interested in the director than in the stars of the film. Who was the young man who had made such a new and different kind of film? Across the Atlantic Ocean, people in America were asking the same question. Alfred Hitchcock and *The Lodger* were scaring people there, too.

Hitch and Alma returned to England after their honeymoon. Everyone was talking about Alfred Hitchcock, Britain's first great movie director.

Hitch was eager to make more movies, but he didn't always like the ones he was asked to direct. Sometimes he got bored on the set and played pranks on the cast and crew. Once he sent an actress four hundred smoked herring. Her whole house smelled like fish for weeks!

Another time he had a horse delivered to an
actor's dressing room for no reason! Alma
sometimes worried that people would get angry
at her husband for his pranks at work.

The following January, Alma had exciting news for Hitch. She was going to have a baby. Things were always fun at the Hitchcock home. They entertained often at their apartment in London. They had big dinner parties filled with friends and famous people. Hitch loved to eat and drink. He was a big man and getting bigger all the time.

Hitch and Alma bought a country house in the village of Shamley Green. Their house was called Winter's Grace. It had large gardens and a brook. They would spend the week working in London and then relax in the quiet countryside on the weekends. Every Sunday, Hitch and Alma attended mass at the local church. It was a very happy time for the Hitchcock family.

Hitch and Alma's daughter, Patricia Hitchcock, was born July 7, 1928, at their London apartment.

Watching and waiting for Alma to have a baby was so scary for Hitch that he ran out of the building and disappeared for hours. When he came home, he brought Alma a new sapphire-and-gold bracelet to make up for running away.

"I wasn't really feeling bad at all," Alma told him.

"I know *you* weren't, my dear," Hitch said. "But consider *my* suffering. I nearly died of the suspense!"

At first Hitch was even afraid to touch his daughter, but he soon grew to love her just as much as Alma.

The same year Pat Hitchcock was born, "talkies"—movies with sound—took the world by storm. Hitch already had plans for his first talking movie. *Blackmail* was a tale of secrets, betrayal, and murder.

Chapter 4
Britain's Great Director

In an important scene from *Blackmail,* a young girl joins her family for breakfast. Then a neighbor arrives to gossip about a terrible murder that happened the night before. The girl is the killer, but no one suspects this. As the neighbor chatters on, her voice becomes more and more distorted except when she repeats the word KNIFE. That single word is repeated over and over, loud and clear.

This creative use of sound forced the audience to feel what the girl was feeling. They understood her horror and shame at what she had done. Once again Alfred Hitchcock was demonstrating new and exciting ways of making movies. He used sound as creatively as he had used camera angles and visual details in his previous films.

Blackmail was a hit. Hitch's home life was happy. Patricia was bright and funny. Alma, whom he called "Madam," was his best friend and favorite professional partner. He trusted her opinion above anyone else's. Alma also helped write many of his scripts.

In 1934, Michael Balcon again found a perfect script for the great director. *The Man Who Knew Too Much* was the story of a couple on vacation whose child is kidnapped when they're mistaken for spies.

It was a huge hit in England.

Hitch followed it with other exciting movies: *The 39 Steps*, *Secret Agent*—the story of a British spy—and *Sabotage*, in which a young wife comes to realize her husband is a terrorist.

All these films portray characters who have been wrongly accused and who are in danger. Hitchcock loved to make audiences wonder what was going to happen next and who the real villain was.

Pat Hitchcock was also getting interested in her famous father's work. By the time she was eight, she wanted to be an actress. At her boarding school she was cast in the school play. Another film director, Alexander Korda, actually offered her a movie contract as a joke on her father, who was his rival. Although she was away at boarding school in Sussex, Pat saw her parents a lot. On weekends they visited the school or brought her home to Shamley Green. Pat loved listening to her father's jokes and impressions of the actors he worked with. And young Pat was Hitch's favorite audience.

By this time, Hitchcock's movies were big hits both at home in England and in the United States.

But Hitch had never been to America. In 1937, he, Alma, and Pat arrived in New York City.

He was already famous for his hit movies, and the press in New York couldn't get enough of the larger-than-life Hitchcock. In person he was very

funny and very large. One night he went to the
21 Club and ate three steak dinners and three ice
cream sundaes in one sitting. The press reported
every bite.

The Hitchcocks traveled around New York State for two weeks. That was long enough for Hitch to see that he could be happy living in America.

Back home in London, Hitchcock's latest film, *The Lady Vanishes*, was another hit. David O. Selznick, a film producer in Hollywood, wanted to meet the exciting British director and bring him to California. The Hitchcock family returned to the United States in June 1938. This time they traveled to the West Coast, where Hitch made a deal to work with Selznick. The Hitchcocks—along with their two dogs, Edward IX and Mr. Jenkins—were moving to Hollywood.

Chapter 5
Hello, Hollywood

There were already many British directors, writers, and actors in Hollywood when the Hitchcocks arrived in 1939. But Hitch preferred the company of Americans like his new movie star neighbors, Clark Gable and Carole Lombard.

Hitch's early days in Hollywood were focused on making his first American movie, *Rebecca*, starring Joan Fontaine and Lawrence Olivier.

World War II was close to breaking out in Europe. Soon England, especially London, would be the target of German bomber planes.

CLARK GABLE
AND CAROLE LOMBARD

CLARK GABLE (1901–1960) WAS A LEADING MAN IN OVER SIXTY MOVIES FROM 1931 UNTIL HIS DEATH IN 1960. PERHAPS KNOWN BEST FOR HIS ROLE AS RHETT BUTLER IN *GONE WITH THE WIND*, HIS FINAL LINE IN THAT FILM IS ONE OF THE MOST FAMOUS IN MOVIE HISTORY: "FRANKLY, MY DEAR, I DON'T GIVE A DAMN."

CAROLE LOMBARD (1908–1942) WAS THE HIGHEST-PAID STAR IN HOLLYWOOD IN THE LATE 1930S. SHE WAS KNOWN FOR HER QUICK TIMING IN COMEDIC ROLES AND FAMOUS PRANKS.

GABLE AND LOMBARD STARRED IN A MOVIE TOGETHER IN 1932 AND WERE MARRIED IN 1939. IN 1942, CAROLE'S PLANE CRASHED IN THE MOUNTAINS OF NEVADA. CLARK WAS NEVER QUITE THE SAME AFTER HER DEATH.

Hitch's old friend and boss Michael Balcon called Hitch a "deserter" for leaving England, but the British government was grateful for artists like Hitchcock working in Hollywood. Even movies that weren't about the war were often seen as promoting a brave British attitude.

Rebecca premiered in Hollywood in 1940. At the Academy Awards in 1941, Hitchcock was nominated for Best Director, and *Rebecca* won the Oscar for Best Picture of the Year. His first American movie had won the biggest prize of all—it hadn't taken Hitch long to conquer Hollywood.

At age thirteen, Hitch's daughter, Pat, was cast in a play on Broadway. The play was called *Solitaire*. Hitch and Alma were very proud of her success.

Alma went to New York for the play's opening night, but Hitch had to stay in Hollywood and work. Pat didn't mind. She said she would be more nervous with her father in the audience watching!

On September 26, 1942, Hitch's elderly mother died. And only a few months later, his brother, William, died unexpectedly of heart failure. His sister had moved to South Africa. Now Hitch had no family left in England.

In many ways Hitchcock's next movie, *Shadow of a Doubt,* was a tribute to his mother. Most of the mothers in Hitch's films were a little bit scary, but the mother in this film is written with great affection. Hitchcock more than once said that *Shadow of a Doubt* was one of his favorite pictures. He loved the story of the typical American family in a typical small American town . . . with a little murder thrown in.

Chapter 6
War

Alfred Hitchcock was always a large man. He had once weighed as much as 365 pounds. But in the early 1940s, he went on an extreme diet. He lost over 150 pounds.

Even so, he wasn't in the best of health. He had heart damage and a hernia—a rupture in his stomach. Although he knew he should, Hitch refused to have the necessary surgery to treat it.

After filming *Lifeboat* in 1944, Hitch and Alma traveled to England, where Hitch made two short films about the war for the British government.

The government hoped the movies would give courage and support to the brave French people who were fighting to free their country from the Nazis.

For Hitch, the return to England was bittersweet. Not only was his family gone, but his home city of London had been devastated by bombs.

THE BLITZ

   BLITZ IS THE GERMAN WORD FOR LIGHTNING.
"THE BLITZ" REFERS TO GERMANY'S PLAN TO BOMB
THE UNITED KINGDOM INTO SUBMISSION DURING
WORLD WAR II. STARTING ON SEPTEMBER 7, 1940,
SIXTEEN BRITISH CITIES WERE BOMBED FOR
FIFTY-SEVEN CONSECUTIVE NIGHTS. MORE THAN
ONE MILLION HOMES IN LONDON WERE DAMAGED
OR DESTROYED, AND OVER FORTY THOUSAND
PEOPLE WERE KILLED. MANY LONDONERS FLED THE
CITY. SOME SENT THEIR CHILDREN AWAY FROM
THE DANGER TO THE BRITISH COUNTRYSIDE OR
EVEN TO OTHER COUNTRIES.

When they returned to the United States, Alma applied for American citizenship for herself and Pat. Hitchcock chose to remain a British citizen.

Hitch's contract with his producer, David O. Selznick, ended in 1947, and Hitch decided to produce his next film himself. His first color film, *Rope*, was shot entirely in long, ten-minute scenes. Most movies are made up of short shots of five to fifteen seconds each.

Hitchcock produced two movies on his own, and neither were hits. Although his movies were known all over the world, his reputation as a master was slipping. But then, in April 1950, he read a novel by

Patricia Highsmith: *Strangers on a Train*.

FROM BLACK AND WHITE TO COLOR

OUT OF THE TEN MOVIES NOMINATED FOR BEST PICTURE OF THE YEAR IN 1939, ONLY THE WINNER, *GONE WITH THE WIND*, WAS FILMED ENTIRELY IN COLOR. THE OTHER NINE WERE ALL SHOT IN BLACK AND WHITE, EXCEPT FOR *THE WIZARD OF OZ*, WHICH WAS FILMED PARTLY IN BLACK AND WHITE AND PARTLY IN COLOR. ALTHOUGH THE FIRST TECHNICOLOR FEATURE FILM WAS RELEASED IN 1935, THE FILM WAS EXPENSIVE AND CUMBERSOME TO WORK WITH. IT WASN'T UNTIL TECHNICOLOR DEVELOPED ITS SUPERIOR COLOR PRINTS IN 1955 THAT DIRECTORS BEGAN TO PREFER THE NEW COLOR FILM. ALTHOUGH HITCHCOCK USED COLOR FILM FOR *ROPE* IN 1948, HE STILL SHOT FILMS IN BLACK AND WHITE AS LATE AS 1960.

In the story, two strangers, Guy and Bruno,
meet on a train. Bruno jokes about the perfect
murder. Guy laughs off the idea—until Bruno
puts the plan in motion.

Crime was a popular subject in movies at the time. But many crime films were considered only "B" movies—the second, less important half of a double feature. Hitch's crime movies were special. They gave people something to think about.

YOU'LL talk to your Friends about it!
BUT you'll Never talk to...
STRANGERS ON A TRAIN!

PATRICIA HIGHSMITH (1921–1995)

BORN IN TEXAS AND RAISED IN NEW YORK CITY, PATRICIA HIGHSMITH WROTE SUSPENSE NOVELS AND CRIME FICTION. AS A CHILD, SHE FANTASIZED THAT HER NEIGHBORS HAD MURDEROUS PLANS AND KEPT MYSTERIOUS SECRETS. HER FIRST NOVEL, *STRANGERS ON A TRAIN*, WAS ONLY MILDLY SUCCESSFUL UNTIL HITCHCOCK'S 1951 FILM MADE IT A BEST SELLER. MORE THAN TWO DOZEN FILMS AND TV SHOWS HAVE BEEN MADE OF HER STORIES, MOST NOTABLY THE TOM RIPLEY SERIES ABOUT A CHARMING CRIMINAL.

Alfred Hitchcock was not like other directors. People knew *him*, not just his movies. When they went to a Hitchcock film they knew it was going to have a certain style, interesting camera angles, smart stories, and a lot of surprises.

Chapter 7
Alfred Hitchcock Presents

In 1949, the Hitchcock family took a two-
month cruise to Germany, Holland, Norway, and
Sweden. On the boat back to New York, Pat met
a businessman named Joseph O'Connell. The
two began dating. Pat had a lot of friends on the
East Coast, and Joseph had family in Boston.
They were married in New York in January 1952,

at Saint Patrick's Cathedral. Hitch hoped that his new son-in-law might work in the movies. That way he could stay close to Pat. But Joseph preferred to go into the trucking business. The next year Pat gave birth to Hitch and Alma's first grandchild, a little girl named Mary. She would soon be followed by a little sister, Teresa, in 1954 and then Kathleen in 1959.

Although Pat and her family visited often, Hitch and Alma were now on their own in their home in Bel Air, California. It was just the two of them and their new dog, Philip of Magnesia.

In 1954, Hitch made two important movies: *Dial M for Murder* and *Rear Window.* Both movies starred a new leading lady, actress Grace Kelly. *Rear Window* tells the story of a photographer with a broken leg who is confined to a wheelchair in his New York apartment. He spends his time peeking into his neighbors' windows. He comes to believe that one of them has murdered his wife. His girlfriend eagerly helps him investigate, and soon the killer seems to be watching them.

The movie was tense and exciting. Hitchcock gleefully identified with the man in the wheelchair. "Sure, he's a snooper, but aren't we all?" he said. Hitch, the boy who had once slyly observed his classmates on the playground, certainly was.

By 1955, Hitch was just as famous as his stars. He lent his name to a magazine that published short stories, called *Alfred Hitchcock's Mystery Magazine.*

He also hosted a new television show: *Alfred Hitchcock Presents.* The show was sometimes funny and often gruesome. In one episode, "Lamb to the Slaughter," a wife kills her husband with a frozen leg of lamb. When the police come to question her,

she cooks the murder weapon and serves it to them for dinner.

Hitch himself introduced each episode, and for many viewers his opening remarks were the best part of the show. One Christmas episode began with Hitchcock bricking up the fireplace opening and explaining, "Santa Claus is always bringing surprises to others. I thought it would be interesting if someone surprised him for a change."

Viewers came to recognize Hitchcock's round face and unique—large—silhouette from the opening of the show. Children loved to imitate his distinctive voice and serious greeting: "Good evening, ladies and gentlemen."

THE BIRTH OF TELEVISION

TELEVISION FIRST BECAME POPULAR IN THE UNITED STATES IN THE EARLY 1950S. AT THE TIME, THERE WERE ONLY A FEW STATIONS OPERATING ON THE EAST AND WEST COASTS. BUT BY 1955, HALF OF ALL U.S. HOUSEHOLDS HAD TV SETS. MANY OF THE EARLIEST PROGRAMS WERE BASED ON WELL-KNOWN RADIO SHOWS OR SHOWED SHORT FILMS, LIKE *LOONEY TUNES* AND THE THREE STOOGES MOVIES. IT DIDN'T TAKE LONG, HOWEVER, FOR NEW SHOWS TO BE CREATED AND BECOME BIG HITS. THERE WERE COMEDIES LIKE *I LOVE LUCY*, WESTERNS LIKE *THE LONE RANGER*, AND SATURDAY-MORNING CARTOONS. AS MORE STATIONS WERE BUILT ALL OVER THE COUNTRY, THE PRICE OF TV SETS BECAME MORE AFFORDABLE. BY 1960, NINE OUT OF TEN HOMES IN THE UNITED STATES HAD A TELEVISION.

The Hitchcocks had been living in the United States for sixteen years in 1955. Hitchcock decided to finally become a citizen. On April 20, 1955, he was sworn in as an American.

Chapter 8
Twists and Turns

Before Hitchcock could start filming *Vertigo*, in January 1957, he had a medical emergency. The hernia he'd long ignored now needed immediate surgery. Alma assured the press that Hitch would be fine and that he was recuperating with visits from Pat and his grandchildren.

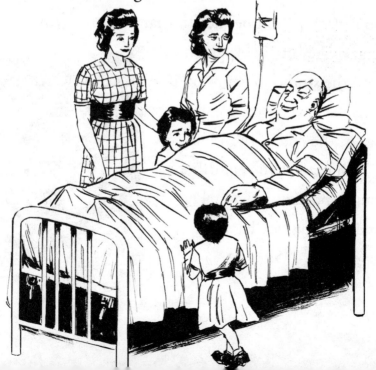

But in March he was rushed back to the hospital to have his gallbladder removed. Once again, filming was delayed.

The next year, Alma was diagnosed with cancer. Hitch was terrified at the thought of losing Alma. He shared everything in his life with her, and he didn't know how he could ever live without her.

Alma's operation for her cancer went fine, and she came home to rest. Hitch couldn't concentrate on making movies until she was well. But he was so nervous about her health that he drove Alma crazy. She finally begged him and the studio to get back to the business of making movies.

At the end of the 1950s, Hitch made two very different but important movies. The murder mystery *Vertigo* opened in 1958.

It starred Jimmy Stewart as a retired policeman with an extreme fear of heights. Hitch's next film, *North by Northwest*, starred Cary Grant as a businessman who gets caught up in a case of mistaken identity. This spy thriller was nominated for three Academy Awards in 1960.

For all the tense thrills Hitchcock was known for creating in his films, no one could have predicted the amount of suspense and horror he had planned for his scariest picture yet.

JIMMY STEWART AND CARY GRANT

CARY GRANT (1904-1986) AND JAMES "JIMMY" STEWART (1908-1997) WERE TWO OF HITCHCOCK'S MOST POPULAR LEADING MEN. SOME SAID THE ACTORS REPRESENTED THE TWO SIDES OF HITCHCOCK HIMSELF. GRANT'S PERSONALITY WAS THE MAN HITCHCOCK WANTED TO BE: FUNNY, CHARMING, HANDSOME, AND ALWAYS ONE STEP AHEAD OF THE BAD GUYS.

CARY GRANT

STEWART'S CHARACTERS REPRESENTED WHO HITCH REALLY WAS—AN ANXIOUS AND OBSESSED MAN, MORE OF AN OBSERVER OF LIFE THAN AN ACTION STAR.

JIMMY STEWART

Chapter 9
The Bates Motel and *The Birds*

One of the most famous scenes in movie history comes a third of the way through Alfred Hitchcock's *Psycho* (1960). It forever changed the way horror movies were made. By the time the knifing scene in a shower stall was over, the lead character in the film was dead, and audiences were left to puzzle over the strange, nervous young man who seemed devoted to his mother. The Bates Motel and its shy caretaker, Norman Bates, made movie history.

Hitch had warned reviewers not to reveal Norman Bates's terrible secrets. Theater owners who showed *Psycho* received stern instructions to not let anyone in after the movie had started.

Posters showed Hitchcock himself pointing to his watch and warning, "It is required that you see *Psycho* from the very beginning!"

Although the movie was quite shocking, it became the most successful Hitchcock movie ever. *Psycho* was made using a crew from the television show *Alfred Hitchcock Presents* for $800,000. Today, the film has earned over fifty million dollars.

One morning in 1961, Hitch and Alma, with their two new dogs, Geoffrey and Stanley, were watching the *Today* show. A commercial for a diet drink came on. Hitch called his agent and told him to find out who the blond girl in the ad was. Her name was Tippi Hedren. She was a model with little interest in acting.

TIPPI HEDREN

THE BATES MOTEL

EDWARD HOPPER (1882–1967) WAS AN AMERICAN PAINTER, BEST KNOWN FOR HIS OIL PAINTINGS OF SCENES OF AMERICAN LIFE. HE PAINTED BARS, GAS STATIONS, AND HOTELS. ONE OF HIS PAINTINGS, *HOUSE BY THE RAILROAD* (1925), WAS THE INSPIRATION FOR THE HOUSE WHERE NORMAN BATES LIVED BEHIND HIS FAMILY'S ROADSIDE MOTEL IN THE MOVIE *PSYCHO*. THE HOUSE ON THE HILL WAS ONE OF THE MOST MEMORABLE IMAGES IN HITCHCOCK'S MOVIE. UNIVERSAL STUDIOS USED THE SET IN OTHER MOVIES AND TV SHOWS FOR YEARS AFTER *PSYCHO* WAS FILMED. THE HOUSE BECAME A POPULAR STOP FOR TOURISTS ON THE UNIVERSAL STUDIOS TOUR IN 1964 AND REMAINS SO TODAY.

Tippi was shocked when a few days later she was offered a seven-year contract with the famous director. Tippi was soon being measured for six identical green suits that she would wear for her role in *The Birds*. The movie told the story of a small town that comes under attack by vicious birds.

It was Hitchcock's most technically challenging movie yet. The director used live birds as well as bird models, and the eerie calls and cackles of birds on the soundtrack. He had to master trick photography for many of the key scenes.

Ray Berwick was the man in
charge of the birds
in the movie.
Hitchcock had
at first hoped
to use more
mechanical
birds, but they
didn't look
real enough.
So Berwick
brought in over
three hundred
live ones, mostly
seagulls. Once
on set, some birds
were trained to land
on the shoulders of actors,
but sometimes the actors had to be
smeared with meat and anchovies to attract them.

The movie posters quoted Hitchcock as saying, "This could be the most terrifying motion picture I have ever made." The filming of *The Birds* was very difficult on the crew and the cast, but no one seemed to suffer as much as Tippi. The birds were unpredictable and frightening, and they sometimes scratched. Even though the film briefly made her a star, the demands of the director proved too much for her. She made only one more movie with Hitchcock.

Chapter 10
Sir Hitch

In 1965 *Alfred Hitchcock Presents* ended its run on television. Around this same time, Hitchcock's movie production also slowed down. It was becoming more and more difficult to find projects that interested him.

In 1972 the premier of his film *Frenzy* surprised and impressed many people. Critics consider it to be his last masterpiece. It was about a seemingly friendly man who likes to strangle women. For Hitch, then seventy-three, the scariest thing in the shooting of *Frenzy* wasn't the murderer but the stroke that Alma had during production. Terrified that Alma wouldn't recover, Hitch almost couldn't complete the movie.

Frenzy's London opening was a huge event.

Hitch saw many old friends there, including
Michael Balcon. Alma was well enough to attend.

Many people wondered if Hitchcock was now ready to retire. "I cannot retire," he said. "I will just have to see where the next body will turn up."

On April 29, 1974, Hitch was honored in New York by the Film Society of Lincoln Center. Many of the great Hitchcock stars were there, even Grace Kelly, who had gone on to become Princess Grace of Monaco.

The highlight of the evening was the great director's thank-you speech, which, naturally, was all about murder. "After all, I'm sure you will agree," he said, "that murder can be so much more charming and enjoyable, even for the victim, if the surroundings are pleasant and the people involved are ladies and gentlemen like yourselves."

In 1976 Hitchcock began filming *Family Plot*, a thriller-comedy about the search for a missing heir.

On his first trip to the set in San Francisco, Hitchcock enjoyed all the fuss when his new pacemaker set off the metal detectors at the airport.

Although Hitch didn't know it, *Family Plot* would be his last film. Over the next few years both he and Alma struggled with their continuing health problems. They spent time with their daughter, Pat, and their grandchildren.

CAMEOS

HITCHCOCK FANS LOVE SPOTTING THE DIRECTOR'S BRIEF APPEARANCES IN HIS OWN MOVIES. MANY OF THEM ARE JUST A FEW SHORT SECONDS OF SCREEN TIME!

THE LODGER—AT A DESK IN THE NEWSROOM

NORTH BY NORTHWEST—OWNER OF THE ALFRED HITCHCOCK TRAVEL AGENCY

VERTIGO—WALKING THROUGH THE SHIPYARD WITH A BUGLE CASE

THE BIRDS—LEAVING THE PET SHOP WALKING HIS OWN TWO DOGS, GEOFFREY AND STANLEY

SPELLBOUND—COMING OUT OF AN ELEVATOR AT THE EMPIRE HOTEL CARRYING A VIOLIN CASE

TO CATCH A THIEF—SITTING NEXT TO CARY GRANT ON THE BUS

PSYCHO—SEEN THROUGH AN OFFICE WINDOW WEARING A COWBOY HAT

In 1979 Alfred Hitchcock was given a Lifetime
Achievement Award from the American Film
Institute. Fifteen hundred people came to the
ceremony. The audience watched a speech Hitch
had taped that afternoon. In it, he told the story

of being locked in the jail cell when he was a little boy. He said to the crowd, "To you young people my message is: Stay out of jail!"

At the end of that same year, Queen Elizabeth II of England named Hitchcock Knight Commander of the British Empire.

The honor was officially presented to him in front of the press at Universal Studios. A reporter asked him if he thought being "Sir Hitch" would make any difference in the way his wife treated him. "I certainly hope so," Hitch said wickedly.

On April 29, 1980, Alfred Hitchcock died quietly at home. The man who had filmed so many murders and gruesome death scenes passed away peacefully in his bed.

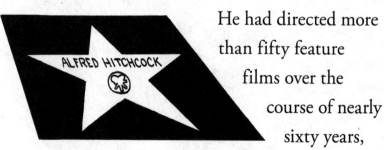

He had directed more than fifty feature films over the course of nearly sixty years, and had become one of the most influential filmmakers of all time. His distinctive style of directing, featuring surprising twists and thrilling plots, shaped and changed modern movies forever.

"The only way to get rid of my fears is to make films about them," Hitch once said. He shared his fears with the world—and the world loved him for it.

TIMELINE OF
ALFRED HITCHCOCK'S LIFE

1899	Alfred Hitchcock born in London, England
1910	Hitchcock begins attending St. Ignatius College
1914	Hitchcock's father, William Hitchcock, dies
1915	Hitchcock goes to work for Henley Telegraph Company
1925	Hitchcock directs his first complete movie, *The Pleasure Garden*
1926	Hitchcock marries Alma Reville
1928	Patricia Hitchcock is born
1937	The Hitchcocks visit America for the first time
1939	The Hitchcocks move to Hollywood
1942	Hitch's mother, Emma, dies
1951	Patricia Hitchcock performs in her last Broadway play
1952	Patricia Hitchcock marries
1955	*Alfred Hitchcock Presents* debuts on television Hitchcock becomes an American citizen
1960	*Psycho* is released
1963	*The Birds* premieres
1968	Hitchcock awarded the Irving Thalberg Award
1976	*Family Plot* premieres
1979	Hitchcock receives lifetime achievement award from the American Film Institute
1980	Hitchcock dies

TIMELINE OF
THE WORLD

Jack the Ripper terrorizes London	1888
First commercial exhibition of film at Thomas Edison's Kinetoscope peep-show parlor.	1894
Martha M. Place becomes the first woman executed in the electric chair in Sing Sing Prison	1899
World War I begins	1914
Murderers Leopold and Loeb, the inspiration for *Rope*, attempt to commit the perfect crime.	1924
The Jazz Singer, the first feature-length talking picture, is released	1927
King Edward VIII of England abdicates the throne to marry Wallis Simpson	1936
US drops atomic bombs on Hiroshima and Nagasaki, Japan	1945
Agatha Christie's *The Mousetrap* premieres in London	1952
Ed Gein, the inspiration for *Psycho*'s Norman Bates, is arrested for murder in Wisconsin	1957
NASA begins operations	1958
Flocks of birds mysteriously fall from the sky in Monterey, California	1961
Yom Kippur War begins in the Sinai Peninsula and Golan Heights	1973
The *Edmund Fitzgerald* sinks in Lake Superior with twenty-nine crew members	1975
Apple Computer founded by Steve Jobs, Steve Wozniak, and Ronald Wayne	1976
Studio 54 opens as a nightclub in New York City	1977
The Pac-Man arcade game is released in Japan	1980

BIBLIOGRAPHY

"A Master's Touch like Midas" by Caryn James. **The New York Times**, June 13, 1997.

A Talk with Alfred Hitchcock: A Revealing Interview with the Master of Suspense. Directed by Fletcher Markle. A CBC Production. 1964.

"Alfred Hitchcock Geek: A blog dedicated to the proposition that Mr. Hitchcock was the Shakespeare of the twentieth century." www.alfredhitchcockgeek.com

Spoto, Donald, **The Dark Side of Genius: The Life of Alfred Hitchcock**. Boston: Little Brown, 1999.

Spoto, Donald, **Spellbound by Beauty: Alfred Hitchcock and his Leading Ladies.** New York: Three Rivers Press, 2009.

Sterritt, David, **The Films of Alfred Hitchcock**. Cambridge: Cambridge University Press, 1993.

Truffaut, Francois, **Hitchcock**. Revised Edition. New York: Simon & Schuster, 1985.